Liar

Jessica Cuello

Cover Art: *The Field* by Leda Brittenham | www.ledabrittenham.com
Designed by Zoe Norvell

Published 2021 by Barrow Street, Inc.
(501) (c) 3) corporation. All contributions are tax deductible.
Distributed by:
  Barrow Street Books
  P.O. Box 1558
  Kingston, RI 02881

Barrow Street Books are also distributed by Small Press Distribution,
SPD, 1341 Seventh Street Berkeley, CA 94710-1409, spd@spdbooks.
org; (510) 524-1668, (800) 869-7553 (Toll-free within the US); amazon.
com; Ingram Periodicals Inc., 1240 Heil Quaker Blvd, PO Box 7000,
La Vergne, TN 37086-700 (615) 213-3574; and Armadillo & Co., 7310
S. La Cienega Blvd, Inglewood, CA 90302, (310) 693-6061.

Special thanks to the University of Rhode Island English Department
and especially the PhD Program in English, 60 Upper College Road,
Swan 114, Kingston, RI 02881, (401) 874-5931, which provides
valuable in-kind support, including graduate and undergraduate interns.

First Edition

Library of Congress Control Number: 2021942208

ISBN 978-1-7366075-3-4

Liar

Jessica Cuello

BARROW STREET PRESS
NEW YORK CITY

for the schoolteachers & librarians

Contents

I.

If

If the father has no bread,
he's an empty pantry, the riddle,
the prank call, the ding-dong-ditch.

He's a voice in the walls, the closet
with its unwashed smells.
If the father has no rent,

if his teeth are missing, he's the bum
next door, the phone off the hook,
idle in the devil's hands.

If he lives next door
with a woman not the mother,
he is the neighbor. If he shakes her

until the bruises and the black eye,
until the police in the foyer, he is the criminal.
The apartment is long and narrow,

a tunnel from end to end.
The front door is a portal to the back,
where a head the child saw last,

saw last. The last time. Then never again.
The back steps are a concrete plank
where he will walk, expelled.

If the father has a first name, is not called father,
if he's a lapse in judgement, if the father
can't be counted, can the child?

Hungur

Hungur was secret—hump
on the back, the something-else,
the body insisting that it was present.
Heavy child head. Teeth in rows.
An assemblage of girl—put
together like a word.
Shame was the time of day.
The body spelled need with
her ugly limbs: half bone, half
skin. Shame to eat. Shame to pee.
Shame to enter in and exit out.
Grown-ups made a body. Made it
like a weed and sent it to school.
The bones grew. The skin stretched.
The body sat in the square of desk.
Hungur pulled. The alphabet lined
the board. The words *That This Those*
were tacked to the wall, strange suns
the head grew toward.

Stumic

Dried dirt on the choke chain, welts
on her stumic, little knots of blood.

Put her down—the dog done,
ears askance in a question to the sky.

Her red-rimmed eyes asked: *Will I come back?*
She came as a motion in the bedroom—

ghost of cold air passing. I reached to pet her,
my arm twisted. *Are you there?*

She did not stop. Paws clicked past
the mattress, her chest a holy hill.

Her stumic had no sores, was smooth
as hardened sand beneath her. Cold passed.

I was not a bystander when her stumic
took the hurt. I was both boy and animal,

huddle and bat. I learned violent's flinch
from her. At night we listened together.

Her stumic was a pillow for my head;
it rose and fell like a cage of breath.

To Loneliness

You're a room with no doors,
the innermost white ash

of the fire, a wool
coat with X's

sewn on the inside.
You are a liar.

We lie side by side

You shape the ceiling face,
sing from the iron vent,

whisper to the one-armed boy.
When the child wakes

in the empty house, you
are waiting. They say

you live in fields of snow
but you hate starkness.

I breathe your cold skin

You are a gravestone face,
a nursery rhyme in the body,

The old man who played one,
who played knick-knack on my thumb.

When the nurse's tender fingers
touch your neck, you cry,

your nerves are pale strikes
of lightning across the silent lake.

We touch with just eyes

You read to rid yourself
of invisibility, and at night,

become a lone tollbooth worker
hunched with fluorescent desire.

Flesh

She holds me to her chest   My baby arms can't grip her flesh

I love her face   before she trains me not to

One of her kind and skin of her skin   She takes no pictures of her babies

Too poor to own a camera she says   In my dress for prom she stays upstairs

At my wedding she doesn't touch me   We hold a little scalpel of hate

against our skin   Flesh of our flesh   Who can say where I begin

Sometimes she puts a photo of a cousin on the fridge to say *I love this one*

that is not you

At Five I Burned Down My Grandmother's Bathroom

The first time I met my new family
I lit a match in the bathroom.

I wanted to make a flame.
It was an accident. Downstairs

the strangers ate and drank.
It spread, from my hand

to the toilet paper, to the
fringed edges of the curtain.

I tried to blow it out
in a panic. It flamed

and grew. The shower
curtain melted. Surrounded,

I shook the knob. The fire grew.
I called out to my new cousin.

Her name was new to me.
Please, open the door! Sirens

came to us. I stood apart.
It was Christmas. The firemen

dragged hoses through the snow,
up the stairs. They questioned me.

I lied like an orphan.
We found this match, they said.

I shook my head, kept
my lie. My Grandmother never

questioned me. She told
my mother to hug me.

Arms touched me.
I ate. I slept in a bed

inside the strange house
that I had burned.

My new grandmother repainted
the bathroom in yellow,

with a flower pattern.
My brother sang *Pyromania*

at me for years after:
Get up, gather round.

*We're gonna burn this bathroom
to the ground.* I kept shame.

Forty years later,
the same yellow flowers

were on the wall, in her shower.
My grandmother was 100.

She forgot we weren't blood
relations, she said, *Jessie,*

You inherited my singing voice.
I was hers. Her last day

on earth, in the hospital bed,
she hid behind the stove

in her childhood rowhouse.
She chewed an imaginary food:

Tastes like cherry.
She talked to people

we couldn't see.
We are going to the icehouse.

She saw people on the other side.
It was her first time going

to the icehouse and the light
was not flame, but growing.

Liyer

My Grandmother says
No one calls my daughter

a liyer, forgetting
I am the daughter

of her daughter,
each of us smaller.

I hoard the words.
I know what speech is,

lines where words go.
I know the vertical line

down my throat.
I read telephone wires

dotted with birds.
I read stove rings

and slaps pink as roses.
I speak to the heat grate.

It whispers back.
A lady comes to make me

talk. I blink at her, bend
my knuckles in code.

I have a debt of words,
a flood. A little bit

is worse than none.
I am the child of liyers.

The lady writes
Self-selective mute

down on her paper.
Grandmother says

We don't know where
her words are

though once I fit
inside her daughter.

House Fire

Who was the burnt man
who extended his burnt arm.
Who were the metal beasts,

swarm of heavy helmets
on our lawn, the covered eyes,
the machinery in the dark.

Our mother carried us one
under each arm, ran down
three flights. Our apartment

was high up—in summer
she poured buckets out
the window to rain on us

and fill the wading pool.
We watched from
the ground. The sky

was lit upside down.
When we returned,
charred walls pulled back

from the frame. We slept
immobile and afraid
on a stranger's floor.

Was it night, groping
and hard, a shell of heat
to separate us. Who barreled

the water, unblessed,
a hard spray. The beasts—
who were also afraid.

Limbo

I draw an eye on my notebook,
a swirl of ink. I'm not sure whose,

but it sees me when
my brother can't.

He lives with us, but died—
somewhere back in childhood.

He won't say how.
His limbs move well enough

to walk to school and back.
I've seen his vacant eye,

seen him in the hallway
in his same sweatshirt.

He won't pronounce my name.
He skips the *i*. He shuts his door.

We once were close, walked
hand in hand. Pre-language,

we shared a bed. My notebook eye
is more alive than he:

grain of paper, welt of ink.
It sees more than a dead boy.

And because he does alive things—
like sleep and eat—I can't mourn.

How the Landlord Taught Me

He faces my mother
at the front door.
She wants heat, like

wanting water. The furnace
in the cellar doesn't clatter.
The grates don't exhale

the dry, hot breath.
I side against my own
because my body

is wrought by her—
heatless, stranger
to her comfort.

I worship the landlord,
with his car and gold lighter
and I'm repulsed

by my own have-not.
Even God's son
saw coins sparkle

when he drew
his first breath
in warm straw.

Imona

I was sick with Imona
on Halloween. I crawled

into my mother's bed—
she had Imona too—

our hot bodies slept
beside each other.

The sheets were drenched.
What we dreamt

climbed out of
our fever heads.

Our lungs rattled.
I dreamt through skin,

a dream canopy above
our lungs. Our rasps

spoke to each other.
Children rang our bell

and called out *Trick or Treat*
though our door was dark.

My Babysitter Karen B Who Was Sent to Willard Asylum

There are only two photos of me as a child.
She took them, she had no child.

She had Kool cigarettes and a job at the drugstore.
She gave me the Crayola box with the built-in sharpener.

400 suitcases were stored in the attic
of Willard Asylum for the Chronic Insane.

She joined her twin brother there.
She wore her black hair down.

A child could admire it.
She bought me an Easter basket,

a stuffed rabbit whose fur rubbed off.
She walked everywhere.

She painted circles of blush on her cheeks.
Loony, people said so,

I mean grown-ups who saw signs
who passed her on our street before she

started to call and say *Remember*,
on the phone she said *Remember*,

Remember the date we killed her brother,
forgetting he'd been committed.

I took her hand and tagged along like an animal.
She was perfect to a child.

In 1995, when the asylum closed,
an artist took photos of the 400 suitcases.

The photos were put online,
the contents laid out respectfully.

In the open suitcases: belts,
pocketknives, Lone Ranger cards,

keys, ribbons, shoe polish,
mirrors, pills, a fountain pen,

bottle of glycerin, a zither,
kit of needles, bread ration card,

The Gospel of John, a letter.
Each suitcase had a name:

Lena C, Lillian L, Mary T
Gloria P, Cassie M, Francis T

Marian R, Catherine S, Dmytre Z
Ruby C, Anthony C, FJL

Viola G, Alice T, Carrie L
Karen B, *Remember*

Imaginary Saint

I collect relics after rain:
the polished bone of bird,
the rag of leaf.

From these I might
construct a boy.
That's closer to prayer

than the woman at home
who kneels before
our bright blue screen

and is afraid of touch.
I summon the face
of a saint-like boy.

I hang my body
out the bus window
and watch him

walk from sight.
I am a pilgrim.
Breath against breath.

Love is the sideswipe
in the hall, a hundred
bodies touching.

I sway with my fingers
on the bone
and leafskin.

The boy says *please*.
Please I say back
and imagine his hands.

I Nod When the School's Visiting Doctor Asks
If I Eat Three Meals a Day

In my family
you recreate *invisible*

and freeze like a rabbit.
You do not cry—

God can read your mind.
In my family, you lie

in the snow and dream
how your birth happened:

the rough edge of the tabletop,
the knuckles of the artist father

who paints all night in a disease.
Then leaves and leaves. No one

confesses anything.
The black and blue mother

scrapes herself together
and into the world comes

a baby with her mouth open.
In my family you tame your needs.

You bite—but don't chew—
the winter leaves.

You drink milk-white snow
from your mittens.

Crusifde Is Over Nurse's Desk

Who put holes in his hands.
Who put holes in his fight feet.

Teature stood me in the nurse corridor.
The red cross symbol was mounted
above the door like a knight's war sign.

When you are nearest me

my hair is teethed by your comb

I'm sent to wash with hush words.
Nurse hands me a papered soap and towel.

When you are nearest me

I breathe

Her desk has a paper crusifde.
A red heart with a sword split through it.

How is the heart so split and red.
How is the man awake to look.

When you are nearest me

hands don't recoil

They stood me there to wash.
They were afraid to say.

When you are nearest me,

sturdy, kind

Like him they crusifde.

Red Fire

Things burned red in the shapes

we knew: dresser   crib

My grandmother said not

to love a thing   but lit

I glimpsed arms   inside the wood

Our first floor neighbor

held his burnt arm

like a hurt animal   I stared

at its red inside and saw bone

that kept us up   that carried us

out but the bone was not

life   Life was in the humming

wound: the red chest chant:

I'm Here I'm Here

The Drowned Boy

The dead boy was a turtle back,
a huddle by the shore.
Police cordoned him off.

He scared my father,
my father pushed
the thought of him away.

My father had his answers:
His *I said*,
His *This way.*

The dead boy was the contrary mind,
my glimpse of lie.
When I started school
with brown backpack,
new shoes, pencils sharpened
with the little hole, I saw him,
dead boy in the forest park
where the leafy
blankets covered grates
It's not a forest, Dad said,
Forests are large and deep.

The boy drowned
in the creek alone.
That day I saw a Heron
fly the length of creek.
The sky moved down
to touch the boy.
Between the narrow
slit and earth

I saw the boy unfold
his skin.

My crying time was up:
Dad said, *Be a man*
and I wore the dried-
face mask of salt.
Wingspan was a fact
Dad hadn't taught.

He hated an imagined
thing and because he
spoke at me too long,
I didn't hear
that world again.

Housing

I found half a house for rent
when I was five   *We could live there*
I told my mother   When I was five

I wanted us together   I told my mother
who had a seizure we couldn't fix
I wanted us together   My brother

had anger fits we couldn't stem   We were absent
from our mother   We had laughing fits
We dared each other   We were absent from

our mother   Our landlord coughed to death
like a terrible dare   on the other side
of the wall   Our landlord coughed to death

slow emphysema coughs   on the other side
of the wall   The faint cry of his wife
calling out his name   woke me in the night

The faint voice of his wife said you had to be married
to live in the house   I dreamt of weddings in the night
So my mother married   *You had to be married*

I got a white dress when my mother married
a headband and a rose   I got a white dress
I lost my brother   a headband and a rose

He came home bleeding not talking   I lost my brother
He pushed out the window screen   He bled and leapt
without talking   He left us through the window screen

I hate   he said and leapt   *You can't hate*   I said
Don't leap   *We live here*   I wanted to hold us together
like others   so I found us half a house for rent

Laundromat with Single Mother

We put our dirty clothes in trash bags
and took a cab to the laundromat
where I gave her the cold shoulder.
The windows were floor-to-ceiling glass.

We took a cab to the laundromat
where outsiders could see my cold mother
through the floor-to-ceiling glass
getting us clean and see

how we got mothered.
Twice she birthed herself
in us. She got us clean,
a young mother who folded each piece

of cloth. Twice she gave birth.
Her clothes and ours touched her hands.
She folded each piece. I buried my face
in the warm clothes

that touched her hands.
I was the youngest child.
I buried my face in the clothes,
I was critic and girl,

the youngest child.
She stacked the piles in trash bags,
ordered her critic and girl
to keep an eye out for the cab.

She carried out the trash bags
when it was time to go
and we watched for the cab.
I was a silent, cold shoulder.

The cab honked at us to hurry
and she grabbed my
cold shoulder in silence
like it was her own limb.

Chiald at the Library

What does the chiald want?
The chiald listens

on the stairs.
Chiald eavesdrops

from the closet,
breathes the boxes,

overhears: *Why*
is the chiald here?

Chiald is thrown.
Chiald is a stranger

in her house, traces her body
in the lot with chalk.

Library has a chiald room,
a giant door. Chiald thinks

soldiers carved into stone
are buried on the grounds.

Chiald thinks
the librarian is Love.

Chiald wants to know
why chiald lives

what sacred is.
Sacred is the library.

Sacred are words
gathered into spines.

At the Metal Playground

My aunt takes out   her soda and cigarette
She shoos us away   We go to see
the dead animal near the sour apples

We bite and toss the fruit
We are shooed away   We put the sour flesh
into our mouths   breaking skin

We bite and toss the fruit   without taking it in
No one asks what kills   We know what
breaks skin   Know what makes the same spot

bloody twice   No one asks what kills
A dog is tied up at the fence   bloody
in the same spot twice   He barks

and the scar behind my knee pulls tight
We spin on the hot, textured iron
of the merry-go-round   At my scar

the skin pulls tight   Someone's head
bangs against the metal   We spin
on the hot, textured iron   unafraid of the dead

but not of wounds   Heads bang on metal
near the dead animal and the sour apples
and I know I will be bit again

II.

Foundation

I turned five years old
forty years ago and sat
on the back steps waiting
for my father   for a visit

Waiting for his last visit
my back to the house
on the gravel steps
where the railing rusted

loose in the cement   rusted
off and the house was
condemned   When the landlord
died   the metal and gravel crumbled

back into earth   crumbled
into dust except the basement
stayed behind   still intact
Even in the ancient

world   outlines of ancient
houses stay   Tourists kneel
on the ground to touch the sites
Mostly they make a single visit

At My Mother's Wedding

We had the reception in Nana's backyard.
She remained apart to say *I am absent*

from this ritual. They said *Your Nana
has a migraine and cannot come down.*

My mother lifted her glass, kept her gaze
level. I wore the dress that I had touched

every day for months. Sometimes I lay
in bed to stare at it where it hung.

I touched the tiny appliquéd flowers. Joy
flooded me for the dress, for the wedding.

At the reception I wandered by the patch
of blackberries. I picked the flesh, wiping

the black juice and skin onto my calves.
I could not stain the dress. The dress hung

in my closet for years though I never
wore it again. Sometimes I touched

the inner gauze that had yellowed
beneath the skirt like a second skin.

I didn't know what the gauze was for,
to keep the dress away from skin,

a ritual that was only for weddings.
I knew what a wedding was, an image

of the upstairs window, a ritual where
my mother's mother was, slanted light

at end of day. Not that I saw her there,
only that I needed to witness, to recall it

later so I could understand my mother
and her absence whenever I felt joy.

That shirt makes you a whore because it's black

I paid for the whore shirt with my own money,
bought it at the mall. It was button-down
and satin to the touch. Who was this whore
that had never kissed anyone, not even her
mother. Who would not menstruate until
she was old enough to leave home, until
she had tasted fat, the pleasure of its depth.
Whoreness must have started at the sleepovers
when we played hooker. We stripped for each other.
No, whoreness started younger: at three, at two, at birth—
in the womb, whoring with balled fists and floating
in the whore sea. When the 11-year-olds played
streetwalker I was the best. What did the best mean?
It meant no smile. It was shame in girl form, which
was shame's first form. It meant relinquish the body.
It meant do not eat in front of others, do not pee in public
bathrooms, not even school. It was the body in plain sight
but hidden—the girl's small cocked hip in the room of girls.

Psalm: Silence

I heard the counselor called your child in
to grieve you and asked instead about

your tattoo. The neck of your child
is warm with brooding, crag child,

rampant with closing. Your neck
was wrapped with Jesus on a string.

They asked the child what men loved you.
Because there was more than one.

Because attention substitutes for love.
Now your son is motherless.

Mary holds a stone body on her lap.
Hard grief. Instead of Him

you felt for Mary, left alone.
In front of the folded stone skirt

there was a cement threshold,
a floor, and no one felt in the way

to kneel on it. *No, we never knew,
or suspected abuse*, your sister said.

Because girls read it right. The instruction
not to speak. Folded knees, lowered head.

Flock raised to be silent. Gulping the rest,
only our beauty made us seen.

The Boy Is My Shepherd

The darling boy is my shepherd. I lack nothing.
    He makes me take off my clothes

and leads me to the scales: numbers
    and numbers, day by day.

He is the motherless darling boy.
    He rides in the valley in the shadow

of the high school parking lot, waiting in his car—
    though he graduated, a former football

star. He is the valley in the shadow.
    He is my rod and my shaft.

With the latter he taught me. He flattered
    my skin—that didn't exist until him.

And the rod was the part he already knew
    as if he'd seen me kneel in church

or heard me take back a word. I didn't know
    how to oppose, so he found me.

He prepared a table before me. His mother
    was dust in the slab of a crematorium.

He was the town's poor poor boy. The teachers
    spoke of his goodness: A role model!

A young entrepreneur! He served me what
    I could eat, or say, or feel. He hit

me rarely. My father thought he was a catch.
        My placid mother made him a sandwich.

I was taken, but I gave. I gussied myself up.
        My cup overflowed with his lessons.

He made me a to-do list for Saturday, for after school,
        a list of people I could talk to. He took my phone.

I was too ashamed to tell my brother. They'd played
        football together. My boy's love followed me

into my days. He said I did not want. He said
        goodness was what I got, and I wasn't sure,

and I didn't know, if I was choking
        on a god or a boy.

House Fire II

Then the gray house of my father caught
again   Some teachers whispered that it
was on purpose   No one died   We got
a lot of money and the school cut

a check for the grocery store   In the house
of my father are burnt rooms   Wet ash is like
paint or melted stone   Glassless windows
are more eyes than eyes   I don't know lifelike

I wore the clothes they gave us   Some I
recognized from classmates   I didn't feel
anything until I saw a bunny

like it was running   stretched out near its hole
and all around the bunny was a mass
of wiry and whitish grass

Sind

The mind sind.
It called me spooky.
It called me by a name

no other knew.
The neighbor boy
unbuttoned me

as I lay still.
His father thundered
once or twice

in his firefighting coat.
He knew I sind.
He squinted at my knees—

down there on the floor.
I sind with my legs
and the school forbade

my bare shoulders.
I sind with my hands
in the devil's workshop.

By forgetting, by singing.
I sind when the school
called me down for dress code

and said, *Place your arms
at your sides.* My fingers
dropped below my hem.

They touched my thighs.
I sind by drifting off.
I sind while gnats floated

with their tiny bodies.
They sind solitary.
They sind innocent.

The Contact Before Surgery

was the hands of a boyish resident.
He came in when I was alone.

Out there, a corridor of Hands.
Hands rushing in white coats.

Hands and the bag of blood,
the cord of sugared water,

the gash to come and my hours
of silence. His hands

circled, hands on my breasts
beneath the thin white gown

that opened in the back.
No one had touched them.

He pulled up a chair.
I know your high school.

I went to the Catholic school
up the road, The Christian Brothers.

He touched the part
of my body not sick.

But I had discarded
the whole of it by then.

I didn't speak.
His hands were between us.

The everyday doctors did not
look at me or sit beside me.

It was an old lesson: hands
and the price of attention.

Green Eyes

Your mouth pouts too much it'll make you witchy
I lifted myself up on the sink to check in the only
mirror but I didn't like to I preferred approval to
the glass how to gather the sweetness her eyes
had for the neighbor girl for the grocer's daughter
I didn't look at myself I wanted to be seen not see
for my mother I unsaw my own eyes which she said
were hazel and I read that hazel was brown flecked
with gold I drew self-portraits I dotted yellow
crayon in the eyes and sucked in my lips to change
their shape saw what I was told to see and did what
I was told to do waited and waited for it to bring me
to her sickness not sick declared I did not want I did
not want no haircut no shoes sew your own stitches
need nothing not a tampon not a glass of water once
a tiny flower pleased her I picked them from the curb
and left them on the table put them in the tiny cup
for juice bought a quilt magazine a thing she loved
I didn't know what else she loved silence no complaints
no face no voice held my pee when the beloved teacher
died I walked into the house without a word and ate
the food and never told hid the gash on the underside
of the foot put the single bra into a bowl of water so I
didn't need another stopped myself from growing ripped
out the thought hated the ones I should hate cut out
grief pretended a father was not there one day and gone
the next never said the name again it was not a gash
on the head the burn between the legs was not a burn
once a man loved me he looked in my eyes and where
could they hide alarm in my chest when he said
Don't you know the color of your own eyes?

Memorizing My Poem for English in the Cornfield

I go into the mass of stalks—

not walls, but wrists and arms.

Some say the world will end in fire.

My fingertips flood thick

with blood. I remember: The Tigris

and Euphrates. *Some say in ice.*

The dirt is cold. I remember

the times tables. Rows like a scalp,

like an organized body. I remember

my father's hand combing lice out

from my scalp and then my brother's.

I lie down. *From what I've tasted of desire*

I hold with those who favor fire. I am

unclean and sleep without a shower.

I learn facts. My father flicks

the eggs and nits into an upright

paper bag. It shakes with wet.

But if it had to perish twice, I think I know

enough of hate. I label the faraway map.

I write nothing on my wrists. I put

the world away. The school bus

suspends us above the ground

each morning. We dream out

into the fog. *For destruction,*

ice is also nice. I free each word

like a white egg leaving.

I'm the Slut

She's the biggest slut
of all, the principal says.
I am. I am the twisted
arms at night,
the baby seeker.
A scalp to smell like a rose.

A loss they say. A loss
for us. How I cut
the arms cut
class
how I make
us leap ahead.
He said he said he said
and she and she.
I am the Renoir girl
tacked to the art room wall
in a haze of gold and cheek.
The boys trade us
as sluts with matching boots.
Pretty bitch, say the boys.
More attention than
we've ever had.

World without end,
a sheet in the wind,
is how I parade in the hall
the invisible made visible,
the unimportant—loved.
All my thirteen years I dragged
behind in sandals that hurt my feet,
all my life they said,

hurry up hurry up.
I hung behind.

How to make the light shine through you.
How a body can.
How to hold the light inside you
and draw it to you.
I bled and blossomed
and now am found.
Now am the foundling
of my own pick.
Now every glance
has worth—
my glowing skin, my soft instep.
9th grade and life within.
9th grade and I am mom to be.
I am the burning station
where love arrives
and everything moves
to the wheel's center
where before I'd been
a spoke
in my mother's eye:
a burden to her.

Irene, Goodnight

The town was not a cradle.
The town wasn't bent on love.

My cousin and I ran beneath
the willows by the lake

until her sister called us home.
The town churned blame

long before my cousin slept
with men, long before she worked

in the hospital where I was born,
long before her regulars

in the ER, the indigent,
lined up at her funeral

to look for her
in her brother's face,

to kiss her folded hands,
to leave their handlers,

to carry plastic bags of cans
at their wrists,

to bang their heads against her coffin,
to touch the flowers,

to not touch, to wander
in the back, afraid to take

up space. My cousin stayed.
I left. The lake had a bottom

they never found.
Irene, Goodnight.

He banged his head on the coffin
and cried for the nurse

that said his name.
While walking from the station

a stranger overheard
her words: *Don't do it.*

Again. *Don't do it.*
Don't do it. Don't do it.

Strangers in the deli said,
Well, that's what happens when.

She worked in the ER
emptying bedpans,

drawing blood.
The willows by the lake

had narrow silver leaves
and the gun was dull.

Her colleagues worked
to save her.

They had to wait to cry.
She didn't die right away,

but he did. It was Sunday morning.
People were in the street

buying newspapers,
buying milk.

Don't to the man who threw
her against the wall

who threw her to the ground.
Goodnight.

I'll see you in my dreams.
We looked at her

in photos on a board.
She was a child and her father said,

Put up the photos
when she was a woman

in pale blue scrubs, arms
around her sons and daughter,

blanket under the wall of branches,
grass in their sand bucket

repeating *Don't Don't*. Not his.
Irene, goodnight.

One time in Salvation Army
the clerk searched me

for a necklace.
I was innocent.

The clerk lifted my skirt,
my shirt. Irene wasn't born yet.

The town was constant.
I couldn't speak up.

Love songs played what
we thought was justice.

High School Illiterate

How did I get this far
Like a secret passed along

My god   my teacher
Why desert me   When my mother
appears in the door frame

she will say I can't   She will ask
for more excuses

My god   way back in first grade
when the others got the words
I used pictures

I am in the white spaces
between the sounds   I am in
the snow outside   am in the sudden
wind that drops dead leaves
in disarray   but not a pattern

Words hem me in
yapping for me open-mouthed

I can count my bones   can peer in
but can't enter
There is no riddle to the dusk
or river   no riddle to the sky

Riddles turn   in manmade
silence   page upon page
and everyone wants me gone

while I wish   to be born again
as the child   who can

Feeding Ritual

Write the instructions in a list:
Rise. Get dressed. Turn his head. Latch his lips.

Trapped inside the breast
is the wholly lost,

the untaught lesson.
The milk won't stream.

Milk is dammed against his mouth.
I listen for a whisper,

for the instinct.
I listen: but no one.

Once I saw a Roman Christ
with beard and breasts.

She was lifting up a stained-glass hand.
But I was late. It was before

I was a girl mother, before
I was swollen and could not feed.

Stuck in glass, always
on the verge of teaching.

Can you hear the hand,
the little sucking. Can you hear

the breast, her sad blue rivulets.
What you can't hear you must list.

The Bird Girl

When a world was in me
I wept for the milk
burning my breast red

red as the wagon in the yard
and plastic things are ugly
when they're old

I took a pill for that
for my child's mouth
smaller than mine

There were seeds knotted
there were walls of me that slid
away, there was the red sea

Before I knit you in the womb
I knew you
and after I was never known

and when the world left me
I wept like Joseph,
father of no baby,

whose wife chose God,
God the adulterer
God loved only Her

Her bird gasp and bird gallows
Tiny annunciation
Nest of the dead

The Girl God

When the surgeon left the mass inside me, his hands pushed

the hard knot and membrane The entire night

she sat upright girl with her mouth wired shut

in the opposite bed who stared through the dark

sipped from her straw and watched me

as I thought I died When they took out the wire

she spoke aloud she became just a girl

in a butterfly nightgown with a giant slushy in her hand

When I prayed on my side she was the god

her eyes were the well where every deity sits

Lockdown Drill During Global Warming

The snow won't fall. The cold is dead.
I have a crush inside my head—where else?

His breath is hot like earth's end. His hair
is oiled like leaves.

Far from violence, they raise us
in it, raise us with an imaginary man

who roams the halls. Raise us with
warm blood inside us, making rounds.

In the corner where the gunman can't see,
we sit, lights out. The snow melts off.

The gases hold the gases back.
The stars pull away.

Satellites float like junk. Thigh
to thigh, I breathe his neck—

cross-legged, far from touch.
The buds push forth like little lights.

We need a gun for a heart rate.
We need a gun for a full-scale plan,

even imaginary, like my imaginary kiss
and imaginary hand,

like my imaginary hand in his shirt,
touching the side of his chest,

like the words ticking
shut inside the picture brain.

I Am the Older Brother and I Tell the Gods

Of the world where we began

Of the stranglehold I put
on the neck of another child
when they called me out of class
to stop my brother,
born as he was, born addicted

Of the blank notebook
no matter what the teacher did

Of the dead snake in my crib,
Of surviving
Of every episode:
Hercules, Hercules, Hercules:
The Called Upon, The Averter of Evil,
The Savior

Of his third-grade teacher who
called me to hold him in his rage
No one else could calm him

Of the weary knee where I clasped him
in his lion skin and let him claw
my arms until exhaustion

Of the adults, who never knew what to do
Of my little brother
Of the birds on the fire escape
who dropped sharp feathers while I slept

Of Hercules on screen
with a loose cloth over his chest
and leather on his wrists

He won and won
but it was never enough

Solgire

To be a solgire dressed in blues
my brother signs over his life.
He's not going on in school.

Below the frame he wears
standard pants, has empty hands.
His upper half is solgire blue.

He writes from Parris Island.
Dear Sister, When I return,
I'll go below, inside the tanks,

where it's dark and small.
I won't sing the song about Libya:
Hear the teacher ring the bell.

Rape her, kill her. Watch
the children run and yell.
The phone rings to find him

at 5 a.m. and wakes our mom.
He gets no issued blues, only a hatch
like an eyelid shut, and ruined song.

After

No one wanted to clean the blood
in the shower, so no one did.

Four days went by. My uncle would

not go in; my father was missing;
police don't do cleanup. At last,

my uncle's fiancé went in with a bucket.

She was new to our country. The death
was not hers. She was nineteen

and went down on her knees. She wore

rubber gloves. A year later she married
my uncle. Her beautiful face glowed

by a candle; her dress was a shiny, deep

peach, not white. No one was closer
to my age when my mother shot herself.

Back then, I used to clutch my shoulder

with the opposite hand. One day she
stopped me, and gently lifted my arm.

Uncross, she said, *Let your chest see.*

No One Is Listening: Psalm 77

I cry to No One to listen.
If No One were for me
my brain would be made like

them. Because who I am.
I am my mother's alien.
How will I hold my arms when I

walk to the board? How will I not
stare at her face, beautiful girl,
since I am my mother's alien?

Seven times a day
the bells call us to rise. Seven
more times they call us to sit,

not pray. I make a tent of my heaven
in pixels and black light. I stay
up all night so I feel blank.

I find my place in the line,
put my answer in the blank. All night
I never close my eyes.

I have never cried or laughed here.
The fire alarm is the single surprise.
It calls us out to the trees

where her face is with
her standing body. I have never
kissed. The name for me is Special.

Has No One left us forever?
Let me remember what No One did.
No One was a god of wonders.

Leaves rustle their underbellies at me.
At night I hear them secondhand.
My heart isn't hard but floats outside

where my mother taps her tentative
hand against the door. I am hers,
an alien. No One tread upon the sea,

marching through deep waters.
No One's footprints are all
unseen. No One made me.

Acknowledgments

I thank the journal editors who first published these poems—
often my first readers & whose affirmation meant a great deal.

American Poetry Journal: "I Nod When the School Visiting
   Doctor Asks If I Eat Three Meals a Day," "Red Fire"
Barrow Street: "High School Illiterate," "Green Eyes"
Bat City Review: "Imona"
Cave Wall: "The Boy Is My Shepherd," "The Drowned Boy"
Cleaver Magazine: "Hungur"
Copper Nickel: "Crusifde is Over Nurse's Desk"
Crab Creek Review: "Memorizing My Poem For English in
   the Cornfield," "Psalm: Silence"
Crab Fat Magazine: "Irene, Goodnight," "At the Metal
   Playground," "Imaginary Saint"
Crab Orchard Review: "If"
Fogged Clarity: "How the Landlord Taught Me," "The
   Androgynous Christ"
Foundry: "After"
The Hunger: "Liyer," "Sind"
Image Journal: "The Girl God" (in different form)
Interim: "The Bird Girl"
Menacing Hedge: "I'm the Slut," "Solgire," "Stumic"
Missouri Review (poem of the week feature): "Laundromat
   With Single Mother"
New Ohio Review: "My Babysitter Karen B"
On the Seawall: "The Contact Before Surgery," "That Shirt
   Makes You a Whore Because It's Black"
Pleiades: "Limbo"
Salamander: "At Five I Burned Down My Grandmother's
   Bathroom"
Southern Florida Poetry Journal: "Ode To Loneliness"

Stone Canoe: "House Fire II," "Lockdown With Global
    Warming," "I Am the Older Brother and I Tell the Gods"
SWWIM: "Foundation"
Transom: "House Fire"

Much gratitude to Lynn Melnick who helped the manuscript
into its current form, to Sarah, Shannon, and Peter at
Barrow Street Press who have treated my book with such love,
and to Philip Metres and Natasha Sajé for the blurbs
and encouragement.

My whole heart goes out to Hannah Vanderhart who has no
idea how often she has lifted me up.

Thank you to Jane Springer and Lena Bertone for friendship
in this literary life.

Deep gratitude to Dorianne Laux for selecting *Liar*. I can't
express what it means to be seen by you. Thank you for your
words in this world.

And finally, to Ed, Gabriel, Carolina, and Caroline Mann—
for making me laugh, for being in my corner,
for adventures—all my love.

BARROW STREET POETRY

Liar
Jessica Cuello (2021)

On the Verge of Something Bright and Good
Derek Pollard (2021)

The Little Book of No Consolation
Becka Mara McKay (2021)

Shoreditch
Miguel Murphy (2021)

Hey Y'all Watch This
Chris Hayes (2020)

Uses of My Body
Simone Savannah (2020)

Vortex Street
Page Hill Starzinger (2020)

Exorcism Lessons in the Heartland
Cara Dees (2019)

American Selfie
Curtis Bauer (2019)

Hold Sway
Sally Ball (2019)

Green Target
Tina Barr (2018)

Adorable Airport
Jacqueline Lyons (2018)

Luminous Debris: New & Selected Legerdemain
Timothy Liu (2018)

We Step into the Sea: New and Selected Poems
Claudia Keelan (2018)

Whiskey, X-ray, Yankee
Dara-Lyn Shrager (2018)

For the Fire from the Straw
Heidi Lynn Nilsson (2017)

Alma Almanac
Sarah Ann Winn (2017)

A Dangling House
Maeve Kinkead (2017)

Noon until Night
Richard Hoffman (2017)

Kingdom Come Radio Show
Joni Wallace (2016)

In Which I Play the Run Away
Rochelle Hurt (2016)

The Dear Remote Nearness of You
Danielle Legros Georges (2016)

Detainee
Miguel Murphy (2016)

Our Emotions Get Carried Away Beyond Us
Danielle Cadena Deulen (2015)

Radioland
Lesley Wheeler (2015)

Tributary
Kevin McLellan (2015)

Horse Medicine
Doug Anderson (2015)

This Version of Earth
Soraya Shalforoosh (2014)

Unions
Alfred Corn (2014)

O, Heart
Claudia Keelan (2014)

Last Psalm at Sea Level
Meg Day (2014)

Vestigial
Page Hill Starzinger (2013)

You Have to Laugh: New + Selected Poems
Mairéad Byrne (2013)

Wreck Me
Sally Ball (2013)

Blight, Blight, Blight, Ray of Hope
Frank Montesonti (2012)

Self-evident
Scott Hightower (2012)

Emblem
Richard Hoffman (2011)

Mechanical Fireflies
Doug Ramspeck (2011)

Warranty in Zulu
Matthew Gavin Frank (2010)

Heterotopia
Lesley Wheeler (2010)

This Noisy Egg
Nicole Walker (2010)

Black Leapt In
Chris Forhan (2009)

Boy with Flowers
Ely Shipley (2008)

Gold Star Road
Richard Hoffman (2007)

Hidden Sequel
Stan Sanvel Rubin (2006)

Annus Mirabilis
Sally Ball (2005)

A Hat on the Bed
Christine Scanlon (2004)

Hiatus
Evelyn Reilly (2004)

3.14159+
Lois Hirshkowitz (2004)

Selah
Joshua Corey (2003)